Brown

**Brown & Sharpe**

Brown

**Brown & Sharpe**

ISBN/EAN: 9783337837723

Printed in Europe, USA, Canada, Australia, Japan

Cover: Foto ©Andreas Hilbeck / pixelio.de

More available books at **www.hansebooks.com**

# BROWN & SHARPE MFG. CO.,
## PROVIDENCE, R. I., U. S. A.

**MACHINES . . .**
FOR WORKING
**IRON and STEEL.**

**SMALL TOOLS**
— FOR —
**MACHINISTS' USE.**

Leading Awards
at all . . .
International Expositions .
since 1867. . .

ENGLAND—BUCK & HICKMAN, 280 Whitechapel Road, London, E
GERMANY—SCHUCHART & SCHUTTE, 59 Spandauerstrasse, Berlin, C. (Small Tools).
GERMANY—G. DIECKMANN, Ansbacherstr, 5 Berlin, W. 62.
FRANCE—FENWICK FRERES & CO., 21 Rue Martel, Paris.
FRANCE—F. G. KREUTZBERGER, 140 Rue de Neuilly Puteaux (Seine).
CHICAGO, ILL.—FRED. A. RICH, 23 South Canal St.

# BROWN & SHARPE MFG. CO.,
## Providence, R. I., U. S. A.

### VERTICAL SPINDLE MILLING ATTACHMENTS
#### FOR
#### NOS. 1 & 3 UNIVERSAL AND NO. 6 PLAIN MILLING MACHINES.

This device is used for a large range of light milling, and is of especial advantage for key-seating, die-sinking, cutting T slots, etc.

The holder or frame is secured to the overhanging arm, and the horizontal shaft is inserted in the cone spindle of the machine. The vertical spindle is driven by the horizontal shaft through spiral gears.

## S. A. SMITH,
### Western Representative,
### 23 SOUTH CANAL ST., CHICAGO, ILL.

# BROWN & SHARPE MFG. CO.,
## PROVIDENCE, R. I., U. S. A.
### No. 2 VERTICAL SPINDLE MILLING MACHINE.

This machine, for many kinds of work, is preferable to a machine with a horizontal spindle. The operator can more clearly and easily see the work and more readily follow any irregularity in the outline of the surface to be milled.

The platen is ribbed solidly to a broad and substantial base and rests upon flat and ample bearings. It is 41 inches long and 13¾ inches wide and is fed in either direction automatically or by hand. It has eight changes of speed for each speed of spindle.

The spindle has three belt and three gear speeds, which, with two speeds of counter, make twelve speeds in all. At its lowest position the spindle is 1½ inches and at its highest 15 inches above the platen. Cutters up to 8 inches diameter may be used in surfacing.

Weight, 5,100 lbs. Floor space, 82x78 ins.

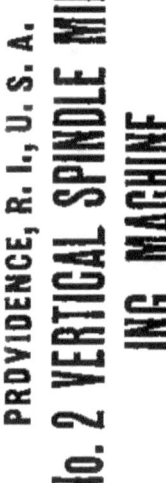

## S. A. SMITH,
Western Representative,
23 So. Canal St., CHICAGO, ILL.

# BROWN & SHARPE MFG. CO.,

PROVIDENCE, R. I., U. S. A.

## No. 7. PLAIN MILLING MACHINE.

The spindle has a smooth, steady and powerful motion. The feed is automatic or by hand in either direction the entire length of the table, and can be varied or reversed without shifting the belt. It can be varied from 0 to 1-16 of an inch for each revolution of the spindle. The table is 72 in. long, 14 1-2 in. wide. Weight of machine, 4,750 lbs. Descriptive Circular with sectional views mailed on application.

## S. A. SMITH,

Western Representative,

23 So. CANAL ST.,     CHICAGO, ILL.

# BROWN & SHARPE MFG. CO.,
PROVIDENCE, R. I., U. S. A.

## MILLING MACHINES.
## MILLING CUTTERS.
## SPECIAL FORMED CUTTERS.

CATALOGUE MAILED ON APPLICATION.

# S. A. SMITH,
Western Representative,

23 SO. CANAL ST., CHICAGO, ILL.

# Brown & Sharpe Mfg. Co.,
## PROVIDENCE, R. I.
### No. 2 PLAIN MILLING MACHINE.

The greatest distance from the center of spindle to top of table is 6 inches; the least distance, 2 7/16 inches.

The Table is 28 inches long, 9¼ inches wide. The platen, to which the work is secured, is 19 inches long and six inches wide. The total length of feed, 17¼ inches. Weight, 1900 lbs. Floor space, 45x45 inches.

---

## S. A. SMITH,
### Western Representative,
### 23 So. CANAL ST., CHICAGO, ILL.

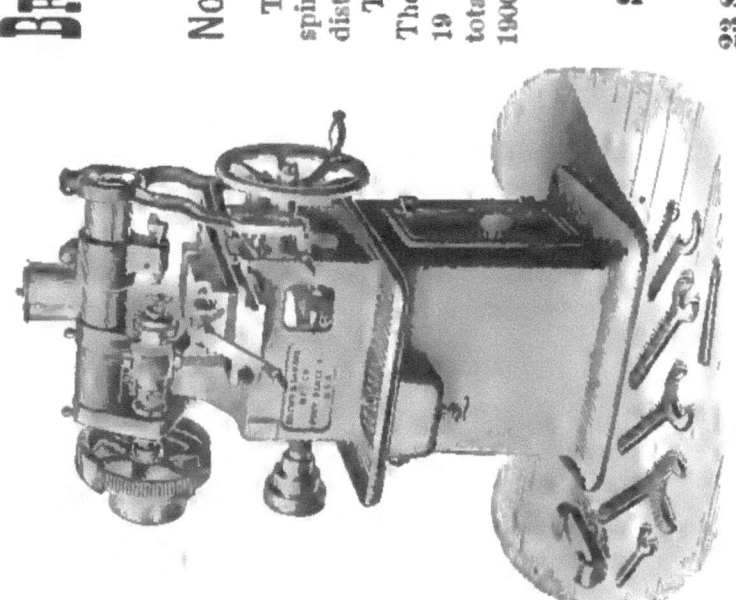

# BROWN & SHARPE MFG. CO.,
## PROVIDENCE, R. I.

## IMPROVED SCREW MACHINE

for making screws, turning, boring and facing bushings, tapping and facing nuts, making washers, pins, etc.

In many instances this machine is used instead of an Engine Lathe, and effects a saving of 25% to 50% in the cost of work.

The spindle boxes are steel, hardened and ground inside and out. The spindle is also steel; its front bearing is hardened, and both bearings are ground. Diam of hole through spindle, 21-32''; 6 holes in revolving head, 13-16'' diam; length that can be milled, 3½''.

Illustrated Catalogue, showing full line of Screw Machines usually kept in stock, mailed on application.

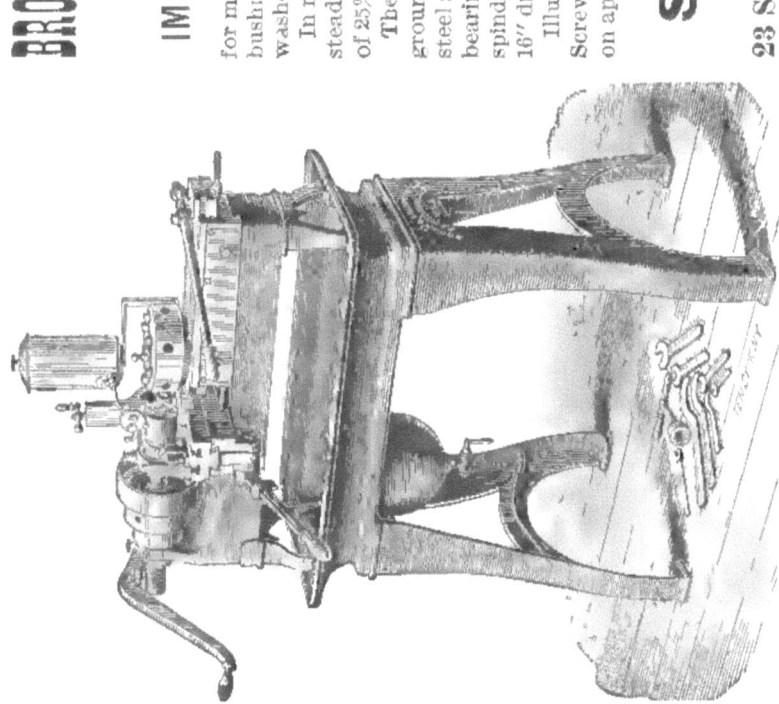

# S. A. SMITH,
### Western Representative,
23 So. Canal St.,   CHICAGO, ILL.

# BROWN & SHARPE MFG. CO.,
## PROVIDENCE, R. I.

## MICROMETER CALIPER No. 75.
### ENGLISH OR METRIC MEASURE.

Patented April 23, 1878, January 22 1884.

This Caliper is shown half size in cut and measures all sizes less than one-half inch by ten-thousandths of an inch. The measurements can be read directly from the barrel; the screw has fifty threads and the barrel is divided into two hundred equal parts.

This Caliper will be found of service to wire drawers, watchmakers and others who desire fine measurements and whose work is of such a class that a Micrometer Caliper can be used when placed on a bench.

This Caliper is also made to measure all sizes less than thirteen millimetres by hundredths of a millimetre.

England—BUCK & HICKMAN, 280 Whitechapel Road, London, E.
Germany—SCHUCHART & SCHUTTE, 59 Spandauerstrasse Berlin, C (Small Tools)
Germany—G. DIECHMANN, Ansbacherstr, 5 Berlin, W 62
France—FENWICK FRERES & CO., 21 Rue Martel, Paris.
France—F. G. KREUTZBERGER, 140 Rue de Neuilly Puteaux (Seine)
Chicago, Ill.—FRED. A. BICH, 23 South Canal St.

# BROWN & SHARPE MFG. CO.,
## PROVIDENCE, R. I.
### No. 3 Surface Grinding Machine.

For grinding punches, dies and parts of machines, cast iron or steel, either hard or soft. The entire cost of files is saved, and better surfaces are obtained at one-quarter the cost of labor usually expended in filing or stoning.

This machine will grind a piece 36 inches long, 14 inches wide, 11½ inches high, using a 12 inch wheel.

Weight about 2600 lbs.

The machines and tools described in catalogue are usually kept in stock.

## S. A. SMITH,
### Western Representative,
## 23 SO. CANAL STREET,
### CHICAGO, ILL.

# BROWN & SHARPE MFG. CO.,
## PROVIDENCE, R. I.

### WORM HOBS With Relieved Teeth.

We are prepared, by the use of special machinery, to make Worm Hobs of any size, the teeth of which can be ground on their faces without changing their form.

By our method of relieving the Hobs they cut as freely as milling cutters.

---

ENGLAND—BUCK & HICKMAN, 280 Whitechapel Road, London, E.
GERMANY G DIECHMANN, Ansbacherstr, 5 Berlin, W. 62.
FRANCE—FENWICK FRERES & CO., 21 Rue Martel, Paris.
FRANCE—F. G. KREUTZBERGER, 140 Rue de Neuilly Puteaux (Seine).
CHICAGO, ILL—FRED A. RICH, 23 South Canal St

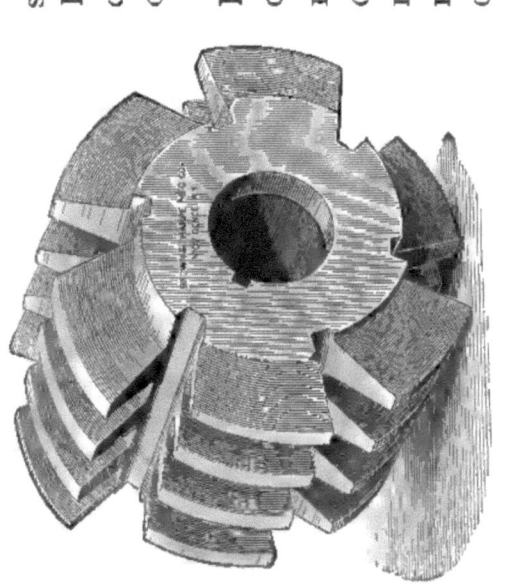

# BROWN & SHARPE MFG. CO.,
## PROVIDENCE, R. I.

### VISITORS ARE WELCOME AT OUR WORKS.

The chief characteristic of our tools, we think, is their accuracy. Especially in this respect we intend that they shall be the best of their respective classes. Cylindrical bearings are accurately ground; plain bearings are scraped to surface plates; alignments are correct.

ENGLAND—BUCK & HICKMAN, 280 Whitechapel Road, London.
GERMANY—G DIECHMANN, Anabacherstr 5 Berlin, W 62
FRANCE—FENWICK FRERES & CO., 21 Rue Martel, Paris
FRANCE—F. G. KREUTZBERGER, 140 Rue de Neuilly Puteaux (Seine).
CHICAGO, ILL.—IRID, A RICH 28 South Canal St, and World's Columbian Exposition, Machinery Hall Annex, Section 13, Crane Columns J, 46 and 47 Center Aisle

No. 2 Universal Grinding Machine—Improved.

# BROWN & SHARPE M'F'G CO.

PROVIDENCE, R. I.

MANUFACTURERS OF THE

## UNIVERSAL Milling Machine

This Machine has been designed especially to meet the wants of Steam Engine and Locomotive builders, and others engaged in the manufacture of heavy machinery and tools.

The essential features and motions are the same as in our smaller Universal Milling Machine, with such enlargement of the whole machine and its parts as would best adapt it for the class of work to be done. The cone has three diameters, each 3½ inches face. In addition, the cone is strongly geared, thus making six changes of speed. There are, also, the same number of changes of feed. The spindle boxes are of hardened cast steel, and, together with the spindle bearings, are carefully ground, and are provided with means of compensation for wear. The spindle will carry a cutter arbor projecting 15 inches, which is supported by an adjustable center at the outer end. Cutters of 8 inches or less diameter can be used. The horizontal movement of the spiral clamp bed upon the knee, in a line with the spindle of the machine, is 6½ inches, and the vertical movement of the spiral bed centers below the spindle centers is 11 11/16. The spiral bed can be set at angles of 35° each way from center line of spindle, and can be fed automatically 22 inches, taking also 22 inches between the centers, and will swing 11½ inches

☞ Illustrated Catalogue sent per mail on application

# BROWN & SHARPE MFG. CO.,
## PROVIDENCE, R. I.

### A NEW PLAIN MILLING MACHINE,
#### No. 0.
#### 16 in. x 4 1-4 in. x 12 in.

(The Nos. 2 and 3 Universal have been previously advertised.)

The table has an automatic longitudinal feed of 16", a transverse movement of $4\frac{1}{4}$", and can be lowered 12" from center of spindle. Weight 770 pounds.

1893 Catalogue, pages 14 and 15.

ENGLAND—BUCK & HICKMAN, 250 Whitechapel Road London, E.
GERMANY—G. DIETHMANN, Ansbacherstr, 5 Berlin, W 62.
FRANCE—FENWICK FRERES & CO., 21 Rue Martel, Paris—
FRANCK—F. G. KREUTZBERGER, 140 Rue de Neuilly Puteaux (Seine).
CHICAGO ILL—FRFD A RICH, 23 South Canal St, and World's Columbian Exposition, Machinery Hall Annex, Section 13, Crane Columns J, 46 and 47 Center Aisle.

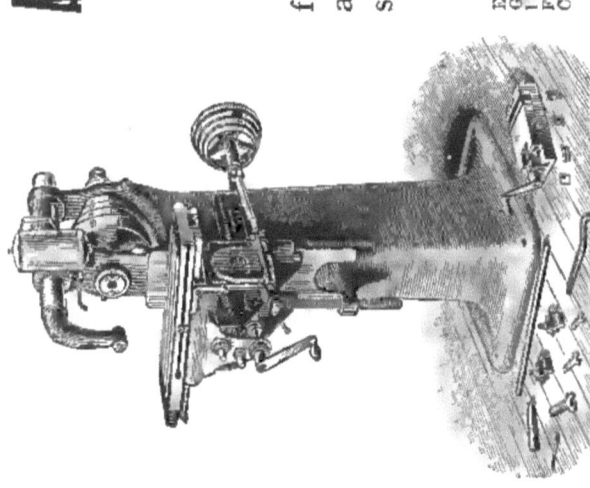

# BROWN & SHARPE MFG. CO.,
## PROVIDENCE, R. I.

### No. 3
34 in. x 7 in. x 19 3-4 in.

### A NEW
## Plain Milling Machine

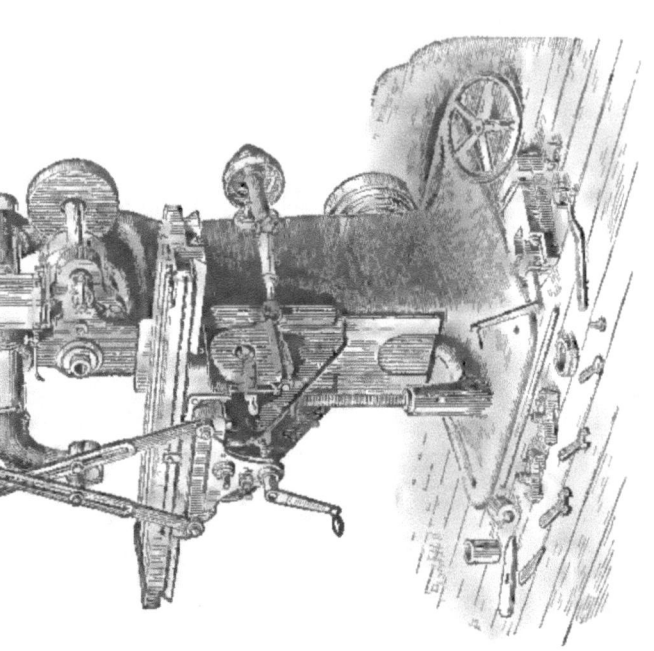

The table has an automatic longitudinal feed of 34", a transverse movement of 7" and can be lowerd 19 3 4' from centre of spindle.

### Net Weight, 2,800 lbs.

ENGLAND—BUCK & HICKMAN, 280 Wht chapel Road, London, E.
GERMANY—SCHUCHART & SCHUTTE, 59 Spandauer strasse, Berlin, C. (Small Tools)
GERMANY—G. DINGHMANN Ansbachenstr, 5 Bnhm, W. 62
FRANCE—FENWICK FRERES & CO., 21 Rue Martel, Paris
FRANCE—F. G. KREUTZBERGER, 140 Rue de Neuilly Puteaux (Saine)
CHICAGO, ILL.—FRED. A. RICH, 23 So. Canal St.

# BROWN & SHARPE MFG. CO.

## PROVIDENCE, R. I., U. S. A.

## MICROMETER CALIPERS.

Price of each, $4.50. In Morocco Case, $5.00.

Patented April 23, 1878, Jan. 22, 1884.

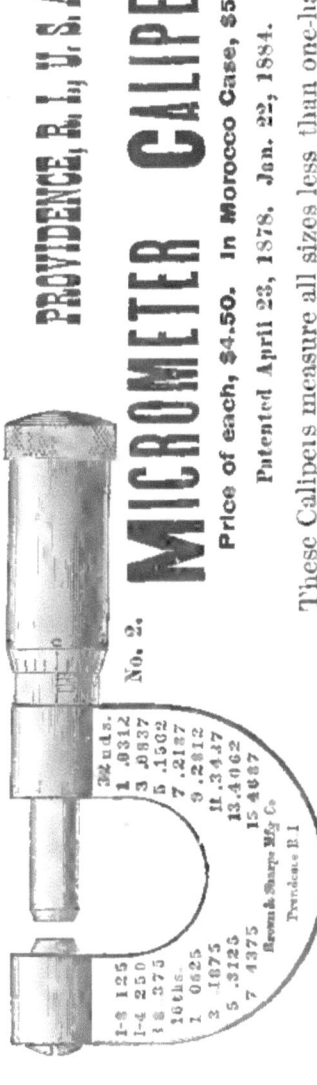

These Calipers measure all sizes less than one-half inch by thousandths of an inch. They can be conveniently carried in the pocket. The No. 2 is suitable for measuring sheet metal, wire, etc. The No. 4 is preferred by many classes of machinists, tool makers, watch makers, etc.

Sold by All Leading Hardware & Instrument Dealers.

## S. A. SMITH, Western Representative,

### 23 SO. CANAL STREET, CHICAGO, ILL.

# BROWN & SHARPE MFG. CO.
## PROVIDENCE, R. I.

### NO. 4 AUTOMATIC GEAR CUTTING MACHINE.

This machine is designed to meet the wants of machinery manufacturers or others who have large numbers of gears to cut. It is arranged for cutting both bevel and spur gears of sizes not exceeding eighteen inches in diameter, four inch face, and not coarser than six diametral pitch (about one-half inch circular pitch). It is entirely automatic.

## S. A. SMITH,
Western Representative,

23 So. Canal St., Chicago, Ill.

# BROWN & SHARPE MFG. CO., Providence, R. I., U. S. A.

## HORIZONTAL CHUCKING MACHINE.

Patented October 15, 1889.

### Other Patents Pending.

The head is back-geared and has a patented clutch for changing from belt to back gears without stopping the spindle. The gears are underneath the spindle cone and entirely enclosed. The spindle and boxes are steel. The end thrust is taken by the rear box.

The turret is fed automatically or by hand, and, as each of the four speeds given by the feed cones may be varied by shifting the lever without changing the belt, the tools may be fed fast or slow for each belt of the cones, giving eight speeds in all. The turret is 9½" diameter, and has seven holes 1¼" in diameter. Movement of the turret head slide, 9⅝". Swing over bed, 15". Length of bed, 66". Depth that can be drilled, 6". Weight about 1,800 lbs.

# S. A. SMITH,

Western Representative,

23 So. Canal St.,    CHICAGO, ILL.

# BROWN & SHARPE MFG. CO.,
## PROVIDENCE, R. I.
### NEW MICROMETER CALIPER.

*Patented April 23, 1878; January 22, 1884.*

## 6 inch, 12 inch, 24 inch.

This Caliper is shown half size in cut and measures all sizes to six inches in length and four inches in diameter, by thousandths of an inch.

The Slide has an adjusting screw and can be set accurately by means of the graduated lines on the bar All fractions of inches are obtained by means of the micrometer screw.

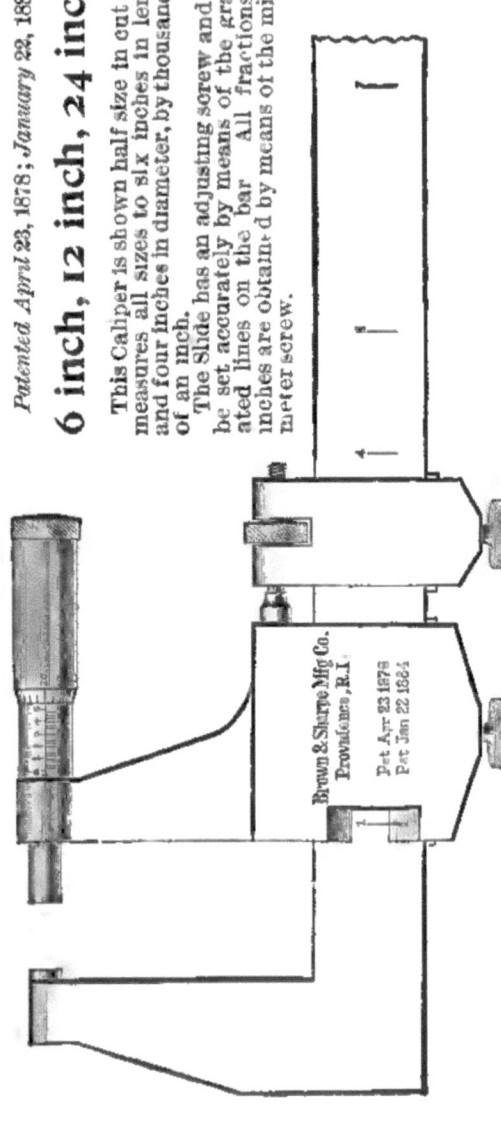

ENGLAND—BUCK & HICKMAN, 280 Whitechapel Road, London, E. | FRANCE—PENWICK FRERES & CO., 21 Rue Martel, Paris
GERMANY—SCHUCHART & SCHUTTE, 59 Spandauerstrasse, Berlin, O (Small Tools) | FRANCE—F. G KREUTZBERGER, 140 Rue de Neuilly Puteaux (Seine)
GERMANY—G DIECHMANN, Ansbacherstr, 5 Berlin, W. 62. | CHICAGO, ILL.—FRED. A. RICH, 23 South Canal St.

# DARLING, BROWN & SHARPE,
## PROVIDENCE, R. I.
## POCKET VERNIER CALIPER.
### No. 680. Price, $10.00. In Morocco Case, $10.50.

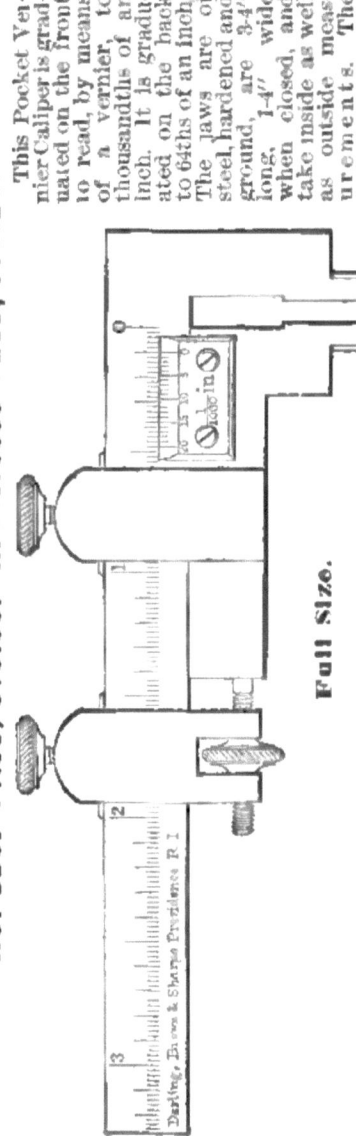

Full Size.

This Pocket Vernier Caliper is graduated on the front to read, by means of a vernier, to thousandths of an inch. It is graduated on the back to 64ths of an inch. The jaws are of steel, hardened and ground, are 3-4'' long, 1-4'' wide when closed, and take inside as well as outside measurements. The Caliper measures to 1 11-16'' outside diameter. This Caliper is furnished graduated to millimeters in place of 64ths of an inch, with a vernier to read to 50ths of a millimeter.

ENGLAND.—BUCK & HICKMAN 280 Whitechapel Road London E
ENGLAND.—CHAS CHURCHILL & CO., Ltd , 21 Cross St., Finsbury, London, E.C
GERMANY.—SCHUCHARDT & SCHUTTE, 59 Spandauerstrasse, Berlin, C. (Small Tools)
GERMANY.—G. DIECHMANN, Ansbacherstr 5 Berlin, W 62.
FRANCE.—FENWICK FRERES & CO., 21 Ru- Martel Paris
FRANCE.—F. G KREUTZBERGER, 140 Rue de Neuilly Puteaux (Seine)
CHICAGO, ILL.—FRED A RICH, 23 So. Canal St
NEW YORK CITY—F. G. KRETSCHMER, 136 Liberty St , Room 303.

# BROWN & SHARPE MFG. CO.,
PROVIDENCE, R. I., U. S. A.

## No. 2 SURFACE GRINDING MACHINE.

This machine is designed for finishing true and bright surfaces for many small parts of machinery, tools and instruments; also for grinding hardened dies, etc.

The spindle runs in boxes protected from emery dust, and provided with means to compensate for wear.

The table is fed longitudinally and transversely, either automatically or by hand.

## S. A. SMITH,
Western Representative,

23 So. Canal St.,   CHICAGO, ILL.

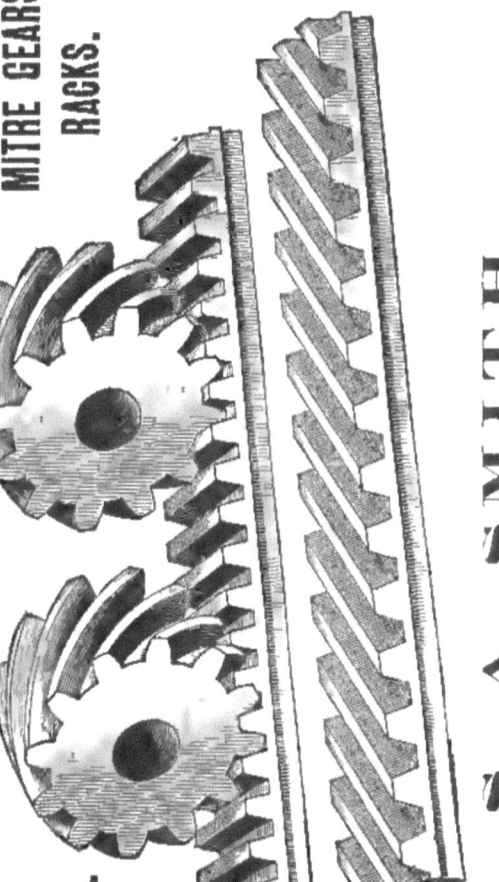

# BROWN & SHARPE MFG. CO.,
PROVIDENCE, R. I., U. S. A.

INVOLUTE GEARS.
BEVEL GEARS.
SPIRAL GEARS.
EPICYCLOIDAL GEARS.
MITRE GEARS.
RACKS.

**S. A. SMITH,**
Western Representative,

# BROWN & SHARPE MFG. CO.,
## PROVIDENCE, R. I.

### No. 1 Universal Grinding Machine.
Patented Feb. 27, 1877; Aug. 12, 1890.

The machine shown in cut has been substituted for the No. 1 Universal Grinding Machine previously manufactured.

The head stock can be set at any angle within the whole circle, and the wheel may be set at any angle from 0 to 90 degrees relative to the wheel bed. The cross-feed hand wheel is graduated to read to thousandths of an inch in the diameter of the work. Work 8" diameter and 16" long received between centers.

Weight, 2,500 lbs.

Weight of previous machine, 1,000 lbs.

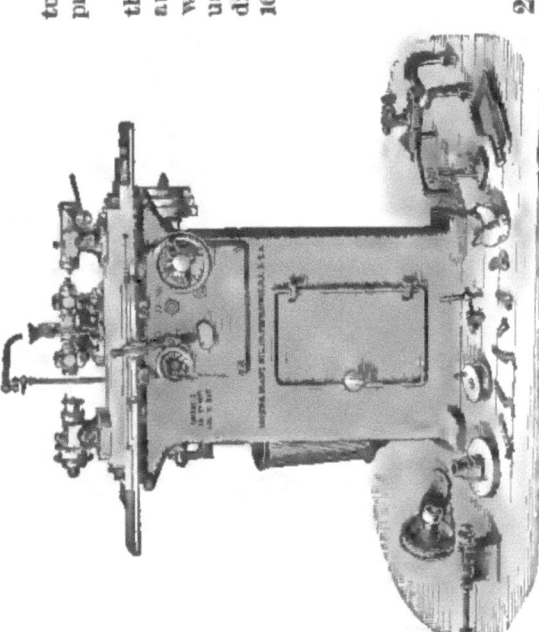

# S. A. SMITH,
### Western Representative,
### 23 So. CANAL ST., CHICAGO, ILL.

## PROVIDENCE, R. I.

### STANDARD REFERENCE DISKS,

for use in setting Calipers, testing measuring tools, and reference for sizes in shop practice.

They are made of steel, hardened and accurately ground to size.

Price of complete set (45 disks and six handles), $35.00.
Single disks, from 60 cts. to $1.50.
Single handles, from 45 to 60 cts.

PRICE LIST MAILED ON APPLICATION.

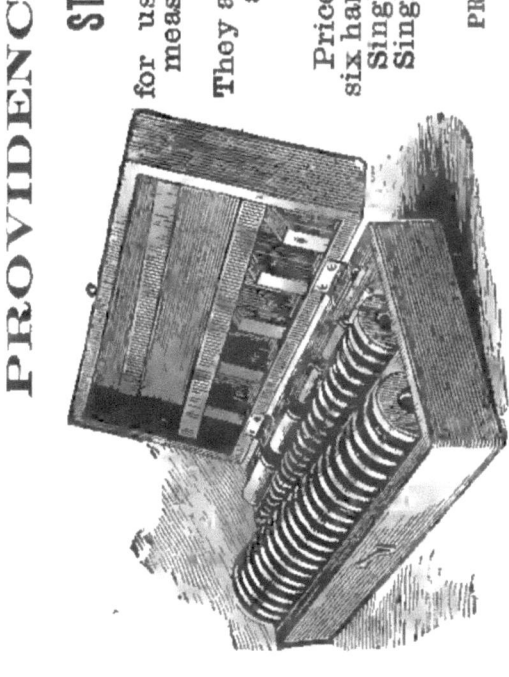

### S. A. SMITH, Western Rep.,

CHICAGO, ILL.

23 So. CANAL STREET,

# CAST IRON STRAIGHT EDGES.

| | | |
|---|---|---|
| 18 in. x 1 1-2 in. | 7 lbs. | $7.00. |
| 24 in. x 1 5-8 in. | 10 " | 9.50. |
| 30 in. x 1 3-4 in. | 16 " | 12.00. |
| 36 in. x 1 7-8 in. | 19 " | 15.00. |
| 48 in. x 2 in. | 36 " | 20.50. |
| 60 in. x 2 1-8 in. | 51 " | 26.50. |
| 72 in. x 2 1-4 in. | 78 " | 33.00. |
| 96 in. x 2 1-2 in. | 153 " | 39.00. |
| 120 in. x 2 5-16 in. | 175 " | 45.00. |

## S. A. SMITH,
### Western Representative,

**23 So. Canal Street,**     **CHICAGO, ILLS.**

# BROWN & SHARPE MFG. CO.,
### Providence, R. I., Manufacturers of
## MACHINERY AND TOOLS.

### Description of No. 2 Vertical Chucking Machine.
#### Patented August 4th, 1886.

With this Machine, from two to four times as much work can be accomplished in a given time as can be done upon an Engine Lathe, and in a much superior manner, the work being more easily trued and fastened in place than upon any machine having a horizontal spindle, and the different tools in the turret-head easily brought into operation in succession, while from the perpendicular position of the same, the chips fall through the center of spindle of revolving table to the floor, causing no trouble by clogging of reamers, &c.

**It has the Capacity** to take a pulley 36 in. diam., 18 in face, and hub of 12 in. in length, and to bore a 4 in. hole in same, making two or three cuts, and finish by reaming, without removing the tools or work.

**The Revolving Table** is driven by a 5-step cone for 3 m. belt, and geared 6 to 1. Steps of cone so graded as to make cutting speed uniform for 5 different diameters of holes.

**The Turret** has 4 holes 1 3-4 in. in diameter, and is securely clamped in position. An adjustable dog allows the locking pin to be withdrawn at any part of its upward motion.

**The Turret Slide** has a movement of 21 in., and an automatic feed which can be easily and quickly changed from the finest ever needed to the coarsest required, it has quick return by hand, and is counterbalanced by a weight inside of column.

Price includes countershaft, wrenches, &c., all complete, delivered f. o. b. at Providence, R. I. Weight, 4,400 lbs.

Illustrated Catalogue mailed on application.

# BROWN & SHARPE MFG. CO.,
## PROVIDENCE, R. I.
### No. 1
### AUTOMATIC SCREW MACHINE.
13-32 in. x 1 1-2 in.

Patented in U.S., April 1, 1890. Patented also in Great Britain, France, Germany, Austria Hungary, Belgium, Switzerland and Canada.

This machine has a hole 13-32" in diameter through spindle and turns any length to 1½".

England—BUCK & HICKMAN, 280 Whitechapel Road, London, E.
Germany—G. DIECHMANN, Ansbacherstr 5 Berlin, W. 62.
France—FENWICK FRERES & CO., 21 Rue Martel, Paris
France—F. G. KREUZBERGER, 140 Rue de Neuilly Puteaux (Seine)
Chicago Ill.—FRED. A. RICH 28 South Canal Street, and World's Colombian Exposition, Machinery Hall Annex Section 18, Crane Columns J, 45 and 47 Center Aisle

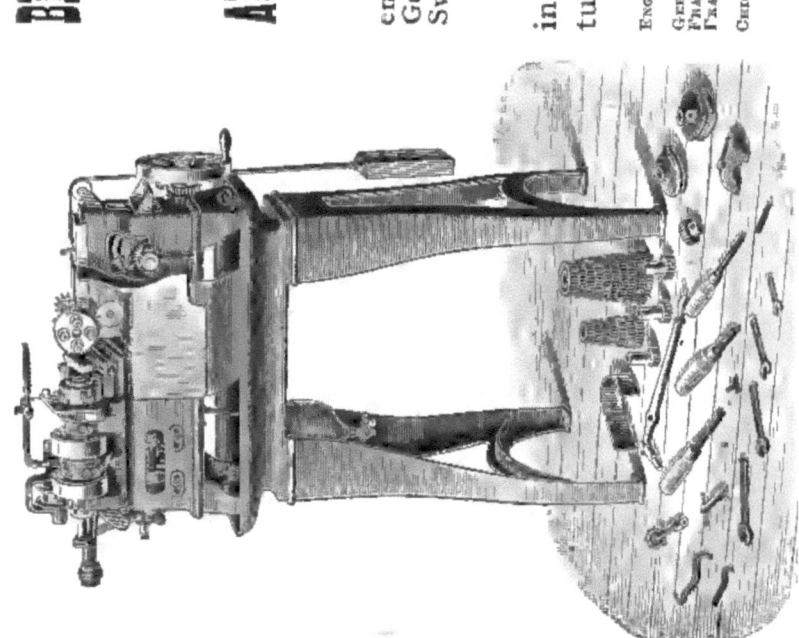

MANUFACTURERS OF

# MACHINERY AND TOOLS

## PROVIDENCE, R. I.

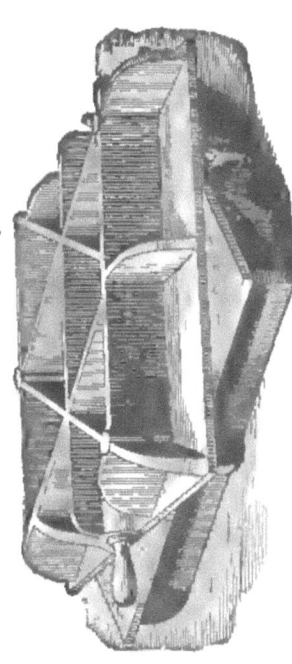

### SIZES OF SURFACE PLATES.

4½ in. x 6 in.
6 in. x 6 in.
6 in. x 12 in.
6½ in. x 18 in.
9 in. x 9 in.
9 in. x 14 in.
10 in. x 15 in.
10 in. x 30 in.
12 in. x 12 in.
12 in. x 18 in.
14 in. x 14 in.
14 in. x 18 in.
16 in. x 16 in.
18 in. x 18 in.
18 in. x 36 in.
24 in. x 24 in.

36 in. x 66 in.

Illustrated Catalogue Mailed on Application

# TEST INDICATOR.

This Indicator is especially useful to those erecting or inspecting machines. It is possible by its use to readily determine the degree of inaccuracy of a plane surface on the top, bottom or side of a piece of work, or to easily ascertain the amount of end movement, for example, of a spindle, or the extent to which a spindle runs out of true.

The upright post, or stand, may be clamped at any point upon the base by the knurled nut. The sleeve which carries the arm may be fastened at any height on the post or turned around the post to bring the arm on either side. The arm turns in the sleeve and may be set at any angle relative to the base, or may be inverted so that the point brought in contact with the work will be downward rather than in position shown in cut.

## S. A. SMITH,

Western Representative,

23 So. Canal St.,     CHICAGO, ILL.

# BROWN & SHARPE MFG. CO.,
## PROVIDENCE, R. I.

## No. 6 SCREW MACHINE.

This machine is suitable for making studs, screws and a large variety of small parts of machines, from the bar, also for finishing work held in a chuck when several tools are required or a number of operations are to be performed. Diameter of hole in spindle 1 9-16". Diameter of holes in turret head, 1 1-4". Length that can be milled, 6". Weight, about 2,000 lbs.

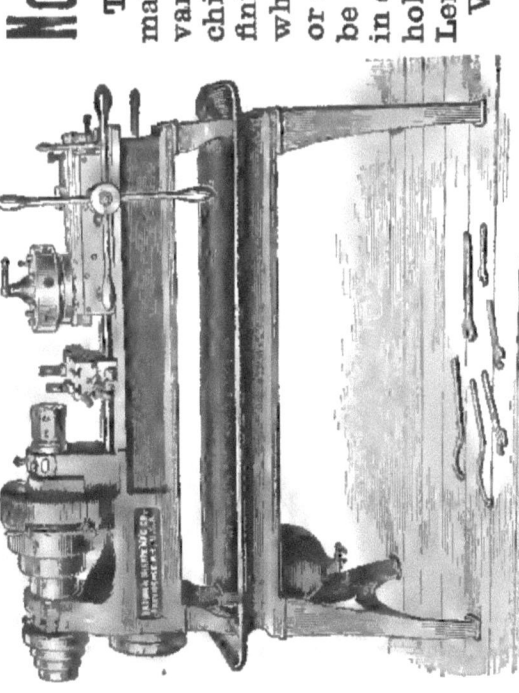

### S. A. SMITH, Western Representat've,
23 So. Canal Street, CHICAGO, ILLS.

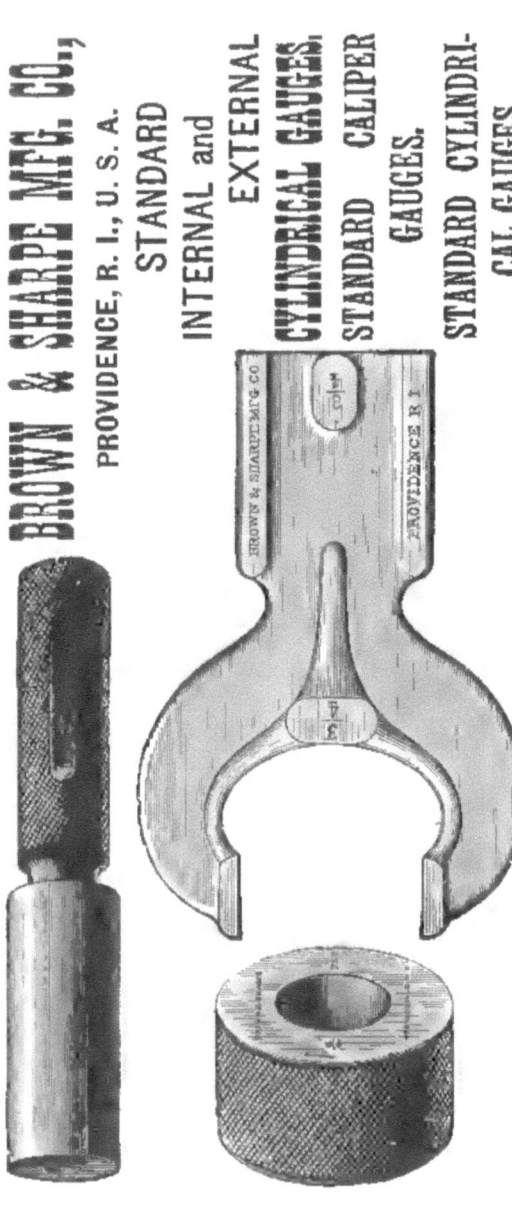

# BROWN & SHARPE MFG. CO.,
## PROVIDENCE, R. I.

## SCREW SLOTTING MACHINE.

This machine is used for slotting screws to ½" in diameter and 8½" in length.

With it a boy can slot from ten to fifteen thousand screws a day.

ENGLAND—BUCK & HICKMAN, 280 Whitechapel Road, London, E
GERMANY - G. DIECHMANN, Ansbacherstr, 5 Berlin, W. 62.
FRANCE—FENWICK FRERES & CO., 21 Rue Martel, Paris.
FRANCE—F. G. KREUTZBERGER, 140 Rue de Neuilly Puteaux (Seine)
CHICAGO, ILL.—FRED. A. RICH, 23 South Canal St.

# BROWN & SHARPE MFG. CO., Providence, R. I.
## No. 3 UNIVERSAL GRINDING MACHINE, 20 in. x 72 in.

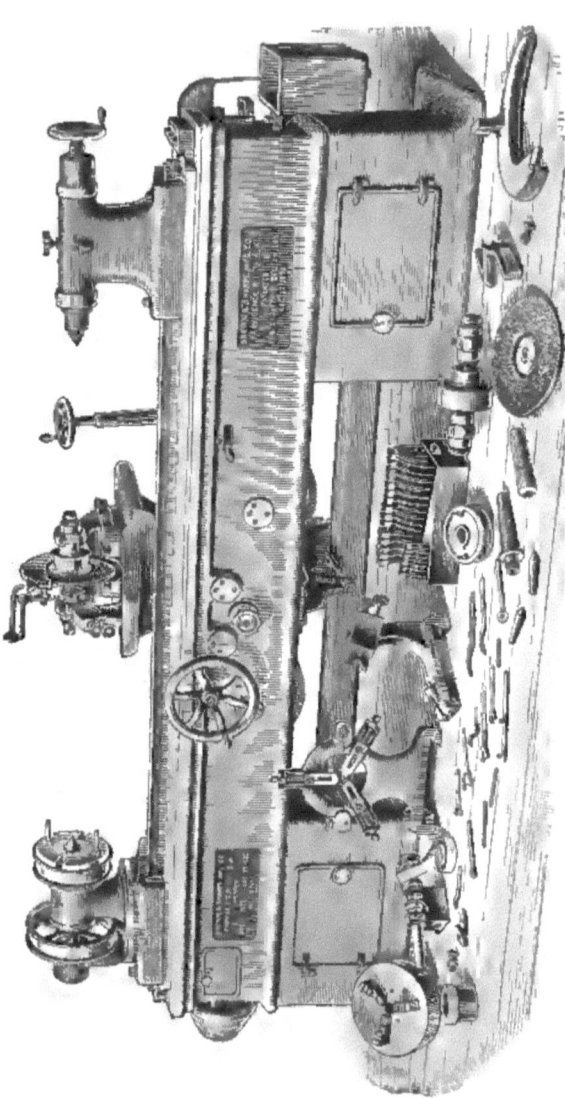

For grinding internal or external, hard or soft, cylindrical or conical surfaces, swings 20" in diameter and takes 72" in length. Net Weight 7,260 pounds.

ENGLAND—BUCK & HICKMAN, 280 Whitechapel Road, London, E. FRANCE—F. G. KREUTZBERGER, 140 Rue de Neuilly Puteaux (Seine).
GERMANY—G. DIFCHMANN, Ansbacherstr 5 Berlin W. 62. CHICAGO, ILL.—FRED. A. EICH, 23 South Canal St
FRANCE—FENWICK FRERES & CO., 21 Rue Martel, Paris.

# BROWN & SHARPE MANUFACTURING CO.

## MILLING AND GRINDING MACHINES.

### Providence, R. I.

**ILLUSTRATED CATALOGUE SENT ON APPLICATION.**

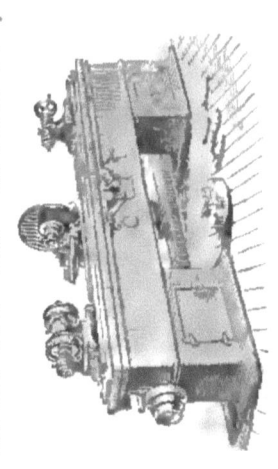

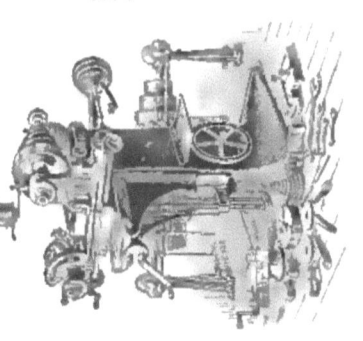

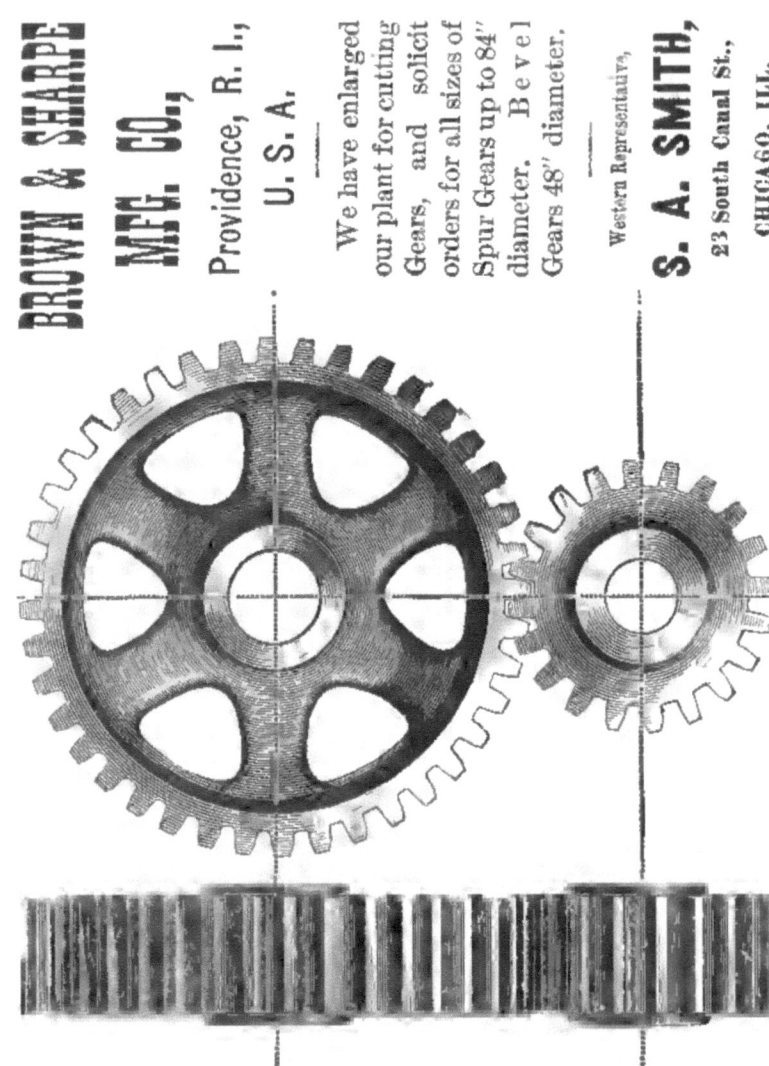

# BROWN & SHARPE MFG. CO.,
## PROVIDENCE, R. I., U.S.A.

### Universal Hand Lathe.

It often takes the place of a Screw Machine.

Descriptive pamphlet mailed on application.

# S. A. SMITH,
WESTERN REPRESENTATIVE,
## 23 SOUTH CANAL ST., CHICAGO, ILL.

# BROWN & SHARPE MFG. CO.
## PROVIDENCE, R. I.

## GRINDSTONE TRUING DEVICE.

One of the most disagreeable things to be done in a workshop is the Truing of Grindstones. It is, therefore, often the case that they are allowed to become quite out of shape and untrue, very much to the annoyance of the workman, who finds it almost impossible to grind his tools in a proper manner. The above cut illustrates a device which is well adapted for truing and keeping the face of grindstones constantly in good shape. This can be instantly applied to the face of the stone, working automatically, without interfering with the constant use of the stone, and does the truing without raising any dust

# BROWN & SHARPE MFG. CO.
## Providence, R. I.
### MANUFACTURERS OF MACHINERY AND TOOLS.

## Gears Cut and Index Plates

**MADE AND DRILLED TO ORDER.**

Illustrated Catalogues sent per mail on application.

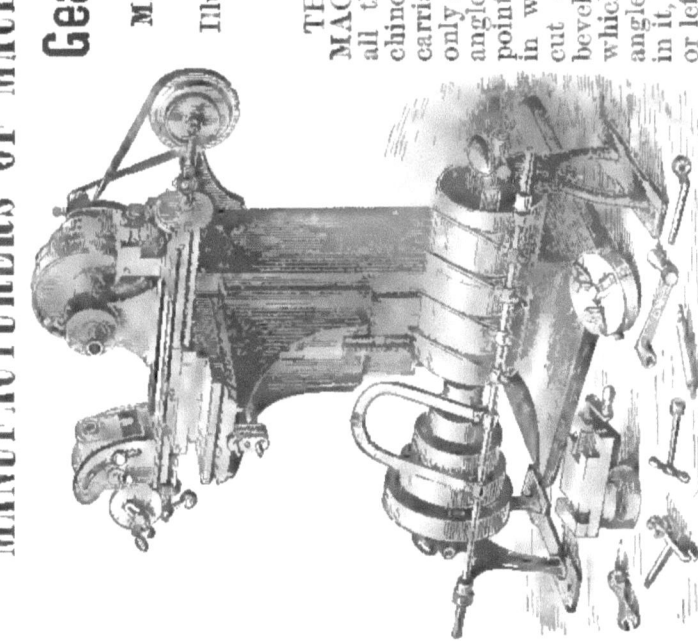

THE PATENT UNIVERSAL MILLING MACHINE, shown in the annexed cut, has all the movements of a plain milling machine, and the following in addition: The carriage moves and is fed automatically, not only at right angles to the spindle, but at any angle, and can be stopped at any required point. On the carriage, centers are arranged, in which reamers, drills and mills can be cut either straight or spiral. Spur and beveled gears can also be cut. The head which holds one center can be raised to any angle, and conical blanks placed on an arbor in it, cut straight or spiraling. Either right or left hand spirals can be cut.

# BROWN & SHARPE MFG. CO.,
## PROVIDENCE, R. I.

## No. 3 PLAIN MILLING MACHINE.

**COMPACT, POWERFUL AND RIGID.**

The work can be quickly placed in position and quickly moved after the cut is taken.

The table is 9 inches wide, 27 inches long, and has 15 inches longitudinal and 3 inches transverse movement. Weight about 2700 Pounds.

*The Machines and Tools described in Catalogue are usually kept in stock.*

## S. A. SMITH, Western Representative,
### 23 So. Canal St., CHICAGO, ILL.

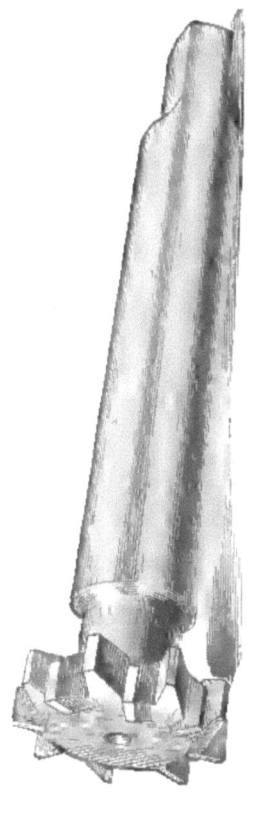

# Special Cutters for Milling T Slots.

## S. A. SMITH,
Western Representative,

23 So. Canal Street, CHICAGO, ILL.

# SANITARY CLOSETS, for SHOPS and FACTORIES.

The accompanying cut shows an arrangement for closets in use at our works for several years and which has given universal satisfaction. The latrines, *a*, one of which answers for two closets, are filled to within a few inches of the top with water, an overflow in a valve in the center of each preventing their being filled too full. The water is let into the latrines through a pipe which extends around the inside of the same, and the pipe, being perforated on the underside, washes the sides. These latrines are emptied once or twice each day by raising the valve by the rod *b*, allowing the contents to escape through a soil pipe. The closets should be ventilated under the seats into the chimney where possible, as shown by an opening at *c*. Special pipes, connecting with upright soil pipe, are shown at *A, B,* and *C*

We are now prepared to furnish castings, either rough or fitted complete for these closets, with drawings showing construction of wood work, etc.

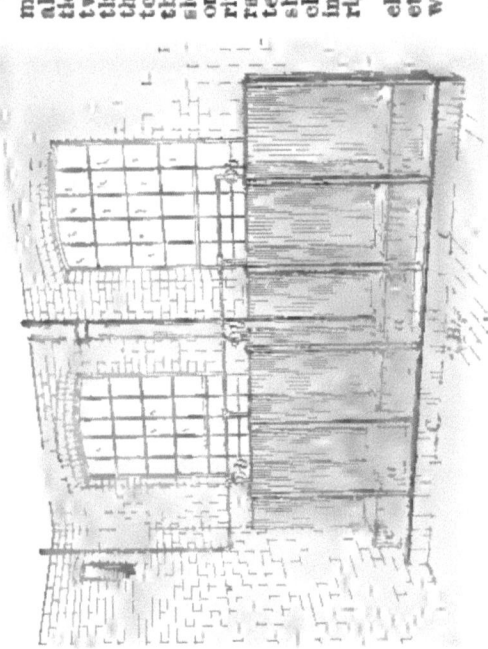

ILLUSTRATED AND DESCRIPTIVE CIRCULAR, WITH PRICES, MAILED ON APPLICATION.

## BROWN & SHARPE MFG. CO., PROVIDENCE, RHODE ISLAND.